Discovering
Cultures

Canada

Patricia J. Murphy

BENCHMARK BOOKS

MARSHALL CAVENDISH
NEW YORK

For Elise, Clyde, and Jasper—*P.J.M.*

Marshall Cavendish
99 White Plains Road
Tarrytown, New York 10591-9001
www.marshallcavendish.com

Text copyright © 2004 by Marshall Cavendish Corporation
Map and illustrations copyright © 2004 by Marshall Cavendish Corporation

All Internet sites were available and accurate when sent to press.

Library of Congress Cataloging-in-Publication Data

Murphy, Patricia J., 1963–
Canada / by Patricia J. Murphy.
p. cm. — (Discovering cultures)
Summary: An introduction to the geography, history, people, and culture of Canada.
Includes bibliographical references and index.
ISBN 0-7614-1725-7
1. Canada—Juvenile literature. [1. Canada.] I. Title. II. Series.
F1008.2.M77 2003
971—dc22   2003019098

Photo Research by Candlepants Incorporated

Cover Photo: Corbis

The photographs in this book are used by permission and through the courtesy of: *Corbis*; Paul A. Souders, 1, 6 (left), 12, 17, 19 (lower), 24, 43 (left), 43 (lower right), back cover; First Light, 4, 19 (top), 29; Lowell Georgia, 6-7, 28, 43 (lower left); Raymond Gehman, 7 (right); Galen Rowell, 8, 15, 42 (right); Staffan Widstrand, 9; Jan Butchofsky-Houser, 10; Tibor Bognar, 11; Wolfgang Kaehler, 13, 14; Ron Watts, 16; Gunter Marx Photography, 18, 30, 39; Annie Griffiths Belt, 22, 23 (top); Anna Clopet, 23 (lower); Mike Blake/Reuters Newmedia Inc., 26; Andrew Wallace/Reuters Newmedia Inc., 27; Douglas Peebles, 32; Earl & Nazima Kowall, 33; Christopher J. Morris, 34, 35; Richard T. Nowitz, 36-37; Patrick Bennett, 38; Bettmann, 44 (top); ReutersNewmedia Inc., 44 (lower). *Steven Morris/Envision*: 20.

Cover: *The Peace Tower bell tower at Parliament*; Title page: *A young boy at a rodeo*

Map and illustrations by Ian Warpole
Book design by Virginia Pope

Printed in China
1 3 5 6 4 2

Turn the Pages...

Where in the World Is Canada?

Canada is one of three countries in North America. It is located north of the United States. Canada is the second-largest country in the world. Russia is the largest. With more than 3.8 million square miles (9,842,000 square kilometers) of land, Canada is larger than the United States. But Canada has only one-tenth of the people. Thirty-two million people call Canada home.

Canada's Jasper National Park

4

Map of Canada

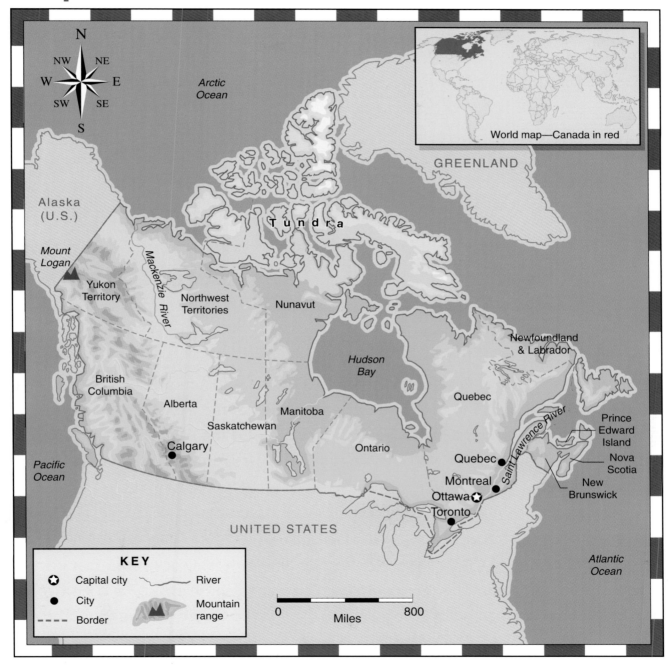

World map—Canada in red

Arctic Ocean

GREENLAND

Alaska (U.S.)

Mount Logan

Tundra

Yukon Territory

Mackenzie River

Northwest Territories

Nunavut

British Columbia

Alberta

Saskatchewan

Manitoba

Hudson Bay

Ontario

Quebec

Newfoundland & Labrador

Calgary

Pacific Ocean

Quebec

Montreal

Ottawa

Toronto

Saint Lawrence River

Prince Edward Island

Nova Scotia

New Brunswick

UNITED STATES

Atlantic Ocean

KEY

✪ Capital city
● City
- - - Border
～ River
⛰ Mountain range

0 Miles 800

5

The Canadian seaside

The rocky Hudson Bay

Canada's motto is "From sea to sea." That is the perfect motto for a country that borders three oceans. The frozen waters and islands of the Arctic Ocean are to the north. To the west is the Pacific Ocean and to the east is the Atlantic Ocean. Canada shares its southern border with the United States. It is the world's longest undefended border.

During the Ice Age, Canada was completely covered with ice. Some land is still covered. The rest is a blend of forests, lakes, and rivers.

In the center of Canada is the Canadian Shield. It is a rocky area that covers half of Canada's land. The granite rock in the Canadian Shield is 3.5 billion years old. Minerals such as gold, silver, zinc, copper, and uranium can be found below the Canadian Shield. Thick forests also cover the region.

Fall in a Canadian forest

On the southeast edge of the Canadian Shield are the Appalachian Highlands. Low hills, *plateaus*, and valleys make up the highlands. Many bays, lakes, and harbors line the Atlantic coastline.

West of the Appalachian Highlands are the Great Lakes–Saint Lawrence Lowlands. More than half of all Canadians live on these lowlands. Along the lowlands, maple trees supply sap for syrup and sugar. Grapes, peaches, pears, and other fruits grow. The Saint Lawrence River runs through the lowlands. Ships sail this river from the Great Lakes to the Atlantic Ocean.

Wheat fields, evergreen forests, and cattle ranches dot Canada's Great Plains. Just west of the plains is Canada's West Cordillera. Formed by volcanoes, the West Cordillera is made up of tall *mountain ranges* and high plateaus. The Canadian

7

The Mackenzie Mountains' river valley

Rockies and the Coast Mountains run north to south. To the west are Canada's Pacific Ranges and Lowlands. The highest peak in Canada is Mount Logan. It rises 19,551 feet (5,959 meters).

The Mackenzie River is Canada's longest river. It is also the third-longest river in the world. It runs 2,635 miles (4,241 km) through Canada's Northwest Territories (NWT). In the NWT, in parts of Nunavut and Quebec, lies the cold, dry land of the Arctic Tundra.

Canadians often call their country the *Great White North*, because of the snow and cold temperatures. Its weather may change from region to region. But throughout most of the country, the winters are cold and snowy, and the summers are hot and dry. Canada's average temperatures are 21.6 degrees Fahrenheit (-5.8 degrees Celsius) in January and 70 degrees Fahrenheit (21.1 degrees C) in July. The average rainfall each year is 29.9 inches (75.9 centimeters). The mountains get most of the rain.

The Arctic Tundra

The Arctic Tundra is known for its cold, dry conditions. Arctic winter temperatures dip far below zero. The average winter temperature is -30 degrees Fahrenheit (-34 degrees C). With its biting winds and twenty-four hours of darkness, winter on the Arctic Tundra is challenging. The ground is almost always frozen 3 feet (1 m) deep. Arctic summers are short with twenty-four hours of daylight. The average summer temperature is 37–54 degrees Fahrenheit (3–12 degrees C).

Despite the cold temperatures, more than 1,500 kinds of plants grow on the Arctic Tundra. Animals, such as polar bears, wild caribou, wolves, and the Arctic fox live there, too. Mosquitoes, flies, moths, and bumblebees are found also on the tundra.

The Arctic Tundra has been home to the Inuit, one of Canada's first peoples, for hundreds of years. Long ago, the Inuit learned how to survive in this cold land. Today, their descendants live comfortably in modern homes on the tundra. They welcome visitors to discover the beauty of this frozen landscape.

9

What Makes Canada Canadian?

Like the United States, Canada is made up of people from around the world. Canadians describe themselves as smart, resourceful, and creative. They are inventors, explorers, artists, scientists, doctors, athletes, and more. Canadians may have different beliefs, languages, traditions, and jobs, but they share a strong pride in their country.

Canada has ten provinces and three territories. Ottawa, in the province of Ontario, is the capital and home to the Canadian parliament. The parliament makes the laws for the country. A prime minister runs the government. The head of state is the United Kingdom's Queen Elizabeth II. Britain once ruled all of Canada.

Canadian dancers

10

The parliament buildings in Ottawa, Canada

Canada considers its name to be from the Huron-Iroquois word *kanata* meaning "village" or "settlement." Canada's provinces and territories could be thought of as unique and independent settlements. Each has a different way of life.

The province of Quebec is a lot like France. Three-fourths of the people are French-Canadian. Their ancestors came from France. Their first language is

Quebec City

French. British Columbia is largely British. Many of its people immigrated into Canada from Britain and Ireland and other European and Asian countries. Nunavut is home to the Inuit, one of Canada's first peoples.

Most Canadians speak English or French or both. These two languages are the official languages of the country. They appear on everything from street signs and food labels to government files. Canadian children learn both languages in school.

12

A warm Inuit smile

Canadians pronounce almost all of the letters of the English alphabet the same as do other English-speaking people—except for the letter *z*. Canadians, like the British, pronounce this letter "*zed.*"

Family and religion are important to Canadians. Most families have two parents and one to three children. Many people practice a religion. Most Canadians are Christian. Many are Roman Catholic and others are Protestant. Canada is also home to Jews, Muslims, Hindus, Buddhists, and Sikhs.

When Canadians go to work or to church, most dress like people in the United States. In cold weather, they pile on warm layers of clothing. Canada's North American Indians and Inuits wear traditional clothing on special holidays or for festivals.

The arts are important to Canada. The Canadian government, along with the national art councils, support the country's

13

talented artists, writers, and musicians. Early Canadian art, such as ivory and bone carving, as well as modern art, featuring Canada's fine landscapes, can be seen in the country's museums and art galleries.

Canadian writers celebrate the country's different cultures. Some pass on rich folklore and legends. Robert Munsch is a famous Canadian children's book author. Canada also has many talented actors, such as Michael J. Fox and Jim Carrey, and singers, such as Celine Dion and Shania Twain.

A walrus carved from soapstone and ivory

The Inuit

The name Inuit means "the people." The Inuit came to Canada from Asia five thousand years ago. They crossed the land bridge from Siberia to Alaska. They lived entirely off the frozen Arctic land and waters. Their homes were made with snow and *sod*. The Inuit hunted polar bear, caribou, seal, Arctic hare, and birds. They wore their hides and ate their meat. Dogsleds pulled the Inuits from place to place.

Today, the Inuit live in the villages and towns of Canada's newest territory, Nunavut. Nunavut means "our land" in the Inuit language. It is the Inuit's self-governed territory. There they make their own laws and elect their own leaders.

In Nunavut, the Inuit still hunt and fish, but they also live a modern life. They buy food in grocery stores. They drive snowmobiles over the frozen tundra instead of dogsleds. They take jobs in government and oil companies. Other Inuit fish and hunt for a living. Artisans sell beautiful works of art carved from soapstone.

Inuit children may ski or ride a snowmobile to school. They study math, science, spelling, reading, computers, and the Inuit culture. After school, they may enjoy ice hockey, football, and string and board games. Like children everywhere, Inuit kids enjoy their time off!

15

Living in Canada

Canada has one of the highest standards of living in the world. This means that most Canadians live well. In 2000, the United Nations ranked Canada as the best place to live in the world for the seventh year in a row.

Most Canadians live within 100 miles (161 km) of the southern border between Canada and the United States. More than three-fourths of the people live in cities or towns. Most of them live in Ontario and the southeast region of Canada. Canada's

Toronto at night

A police officer, called a Canadian Mountie, and her horse

largest cities are Toronto, Montreal, Vancouver, Ottawa, and Calgary. These cities are filled with trains, cars, buses, and people. They are also centers for Canada's business and industry.

Most Canadians choose jobs in health care, law enforcement, education, transportation, tourism, and banking. Many Canadians also work in manufacturing. The rest work in farming, fishing, mining, or forestry.

Factories use many of Canada's natural resources to make their products. They produce equipment for cars, trucks, subway cars, and airplanes. Some factories process foods like meat, poultry, baked goods, and dairy products. Others manufacture chemicals, medicines, metal, steel, and paper. In the United States,

High-rise apartments in Vancouver

people buy Canadian grains, steel, and automobile parts. Almost three-fourths of Canadian exports go to the United States.

Many Canadians own homes. Some Canadians rent apartments. All houses and apartments have running water, electricity, and modern conveniences. In most Canadian homes, both the mother and the father have jobs. Canadian workers pay higher income taxes than in other countries. These taxes help the government provide health insurance for all Canadians.

Canadian cities have their share of problems. There are not always enough jobs for everyone. Canadian cities have unemployment, homelessness, and drug abuse problems. Some Canadians move to the United States to find better jobs and pay lower taxes. Canadian cities also have air pollution problems. Their factories pollute the air.

Canadian farmers grow grains and other crops.

Mining for gold

Outside the cities, Canadians are farmers, foresters, fishermen, and miners. Some farmers grow wheat and other grains, potatoes, tobacco, fruits, or vegetables. Others raise cattle, pigs, chicken, and sheep. Foresters grow trees for paper, lumber, plywood, and wood pulp. Fishermen spread their nets along Canadian coasts and lakes for salmon and cod. Miners drill for *petroleum* and natural gas, and they dig for iron and metal *ores*, minerals, coal, and gold.

A slice of meat pie

Because Canadians come from many different countries, daily meals can be from many cultures. Breakfasts may include pork sausages or *porridge*. A French meat pie may be for lunch. Chinese or Indian food could be for dinner. The types of foods Canadians eat depend on where they live. Salmon is popular in British Columbia. Meat pies and special stews—with meatballs—are French-Canadian favorites. People in Ontario eat beef or pork roasts and pumpkin pie. Canadians in Alberta may feast on moose meat and fresh lake fish.

After dinner, families enjoy spending time together. They like to read and watch TV or movies. They also love to play outdoor sports.

Let's Eat!
The Nanaimo Bar

Named for the harbor city on Vancouver Island, this three-layer chocolate bar is a favorite in British Columbia. Ask an adult to help you prepare this recipe.

Bottom layer:

$1/2$ cup unsalted butter

$1/4$ cup granulated sugar

$1/3$ cup unsweetened cocoa

1 egg beaten

1 cup coconut flakes

1 $3/4$ cups graham cracker crumbs

$1/2$ cup chopped walnuts or almonds

Middle layer:

$1/2$ cup unsalted butter

2 tablespoons and 2 teaspoons cream

2 tablespoons instant vanilla custard or vanilla pudding powder

2 cups sifted powdered sugar

Top layer:

4 ounces semisweet baking chocolate

2 tablespoons unsalted butter

Wash your hands. Gather and measure all of your ingredients. Begin with the bottom layer. Melt butter in a saucepan on low heat. Add sugar and cocoa. Add egg and stir on medium heat until mixture thickens. Remove from heat. Add coconut, graham cracker crumbs, and walnuts or almonds. Pat mixture into a nine-inch, buttered, square baking pan. Refrigerate for one hour.

Make the filling next. Beat butter with hand mixer until it is soft and creamy. Beat in cream, custard powder, and powdered sugar. Spread over bottom layer. Refrigerate for thirty minutes or until firm.

Then make the top layer. Melt chocolate and butter in a saucepan on low heat. Spread over the middle layer. Refrigerate until chocolate has almost hardened. Cut into small squares. Refrigerate again for one hour. Serve and enjoy!

21

School Days

Education gives children the opportunity to learn valuable life skills. It also allows them to develop their talents. The Canadian government requires all children to attend school until they are fifteen to sixteen years old. Each province in Canada has its own independent school system. Education is free through secondary school, or high school.

A Canadian teacher and her students

22

Math class in Canada

Secondary students hard at work

Canadian children begin school as early as three years old. Most attend up to eight years of elementary school, five years of secondary school, and four years of college. Many students stay in school to receive higher degrees.

Students in Canada attend either public or private schools. Public or government schools are free. Parents pay fees for their children to attend private or religious schools.

Elementary schools teach students history, culture, French, English, math, social studies, science, and art. These schools design their own tests to check their students' learning.

High schools prepare students for college, university, or technical schools. Entrance into college

Schoolchildren hang out in the park.

depends on how well they did in high school. Some private schools require students to take special subject tests. Passing scores on these tests allow entrance into postsecondary or college level classes. Many colleges and universities have their own entrance requirements.

The Canadian government encourages all children to go to college. It offers scholarships and other help to students whose families cannot afford it. Because of this, all children can secure a bright future for themselves—and for Canada.

O Canada!

The Canadian national anthem is "O Canada!" It was first sung in 1880, but it was not officially recognized as the national anthem until one hundred years later. "O Canada!" expresses the strong love and pride Canadians feel for their country.

Just for Fun

When people think of Canada, most think of sticks, skates, ice rinks, and hockey. Hockey is the number one national pastime in Canada. Almost all Canadians follow a favorite hockey team. Professional Canadian hockey teams play in the National Hockey League in the United States. Hockey players of every age play on school, club, and provincial levels. Just about anywhere there is an open space there is usually someone playing hockey.

Hockey players battle for the puck.

Another national pastime in Canada is lacrosse. Lacrosse is the oldest team sport in North America. It was first played by native people along the Saint Lawrence River. Lacrosse is similar to soccer and hockey. But lacrosse players do not kick a large soccer ball or slice a hockey puck. Instead, they catch a small ball in a net on a long stick. With these sticks, lacrosse players pass a ball from player to player to score a goal. At a breakneck speed, lacrosse is played on national, local, school, and club levels.

Canada's other popular sports are swimming, skiing, tennis, basketball, cross-country track, and golf. Canadians also enjoy watching their favorite athletes. Over the years, Canadian football teams and baseball teams such as the Toronto

Canadian ice dancers perform at a competition.

27

Windsurfing on Waterton Lake, Alberta, Canada

Blue Jays and Montreal Expos have given Canadians a lot to cheer about. The Toronto Blue Jays was the first team outside the United States to win a World Series, in 1992 and 1993! On ice, snow, and in the water, Canadian athletes have earned medals in world championship and Olympic competitions. Canada also hosted the 1988 Winter Olympics in Calgary.

For many Canadians, playing sports is one way to relax or stay in shape. For others, it is a way to compete—and strive to be the best. The Canadian government spends a lot of money developing its sports programs. It believes that playing sports is one way to teach hard work, teamwork, and excellence.

In addition to sports, Canadians enjoy the great outdoors. In summer, favorite activities include sailing, windsurfing, rowing, hiking, fishing, white-water rafting, canoeing, or jogging. In the winter, many people ski and skate or go snowboarding and snowshoeing. Others play *curling*.

Canadians also use their free time to get away. Many travel out of the

Snowboarding off a mountain in Canada

country to the United States, Europe, and Mexico. Others take trips to Newfoundland, Prince Edward Island, and Nova Scotia. They may also drive across the country on the Trans-Canada Highway to visit national parks and historic sites. At 4,860 miles (7,821 km), this highway is the world's longest national highway.

White-water rafting in rough waters

Ringette

Ringette is a serious winter sport played in Canada by girls and women between the ages of seven and thirty, or older. Invented by Canadian Sam Jacks in 1963, ringette looks a lot like hockey. But it is more like soccer, lacrosse, and basketball. Dressed in helmets, pads, and skates, two teams of six female ringette players use straight sticks without blades to pass around a small rubber ring. The object of the game is to get the ring into the opponent's goal—and to keep it out of yours. All of this must be done without touching the other players.

Instead of a face-off like in hockey or a jump ball in basketball, ringette begins with a free pass. During a free pass, players must take the rubber ring and either shoot it or pass it to another player. The ring must pass over the blue line to be good. Once this happens, only three players at a time can pass through ringette's offensive or defensive zones. This rule requires players to practice together and plan ways to pass and to score.

Today, professional Canadian ringette teams compete in the Canadian Ringette World Cups and Ringette World and International Championships. Someday, ringette may be an Olympic sport.

31

Let's Celebrate!

With many different cultures, religions, and national celebrations, Canadians have a long list of holidays and festivals each year.

Because most Canadians are Christian, Christmas and Easter are two important holidays in Canada. While Christians usually celebrate these holidays in the same way, Canadians add their own customs, traditions, and flavors.

At Christmas, Christians celebrate the birth of the Christ child. They decorate trees and set up manger scenes, or *creches*. They attend Mass on Christmas Eve or Christmas Day. Families gather around dining room tables to share large meals. They exchange gifts and sing Christmas carols.

An outdoor Christmas tree in the snow

32

French Canadians hold a feast after Midnight Mass called the *reveillon*. On this late-night menu are frozen puddings, meat stews, and *tourtiere* (meat pie). Canadian children of Dutch ancestry believe Santa Claus and an eight-legged horse named Sleipner deliver toys on Christmas Eve.

For most Canadians, the day after Christmas—December 26 or Boxing Day—is a day to honor people who deliver the mail or provide other special services. These services may include trash removal, dry cleaning, or yard work. It is also a day to give to those in need.

On Easter, Christians remember Jesus Christ's rising from the dead. Many go to church. They give thanks and celebrate the beginning of spring. Children decorate eggs—a symbol of new life.

A young girl wears Canadian flags in her hair to celebrate Canada Day.

33

Canada's national holidays bring all Canadians together to celebrate what they have in common—being Canadian. These days include Canada Day, Thanksgiving, and Remembrance Day.

Canada Day on July 1 is Canada's most important national holiday. This holiday celebrates Canada's birthday. In 1867, Great Britain passed the British North America Act. This act united the British North American provinces into a new country called the Dominion of Canada. The new country could make many of its own decisions, but it had to follow Great Britain's laws. In 1982, Canada became completely independent of Great Britain's rule. However, Canadians have been celebrating Canada Day since 1879.

Today, Canadians gather outdoors for picnics, parades, special ceremonies, and fireworks displays on Canada Day. Some Canadians wave flags, paint maple leaves on their faces, and sing "O Canada!"

Waving the red and white

34

A soldier bows at a monument on Remembrance Day.

Canadians celebrate Thanksgiving Day on the second Monday of October. On that day, they give thanks for all of their many blessings. They gather with family and friends to eat turkey, stuffing, cranberry sauce, potatoes, vegetables, and pies. Canada's first Thanksgiving was celebrated by early explorers. In the following years, the day marked the end of the French and Indian Wars. It was not until 1957 that Thanksgiving became an annual national holiday in Canada.

Another Canadian holiday gives thanks to the country's war veterans. On Remembrance Day, November 11, Canadians honor the men and women who

35

fought to keep Canada free. They wear red poppies as a reminder of the flower that still grows on the World War I battlefields in France and Belgium. They place flowers on the graves of veterans who died in battle. Some stop what they are doing at 11:11 A.M. on November 11 and remember. November 11, 1918, was the end of World War I.

On national holidays, government offices and many businesses shut their doors. Children have the day off from school. Many Canadians travel to their second homes, spend time outdoors, and celebrate with their families and friends.

Holidays are just some of the events that Canadians

Ice sculptures at the Winterlude Winter Festival

37

Tulips in bloom during the Tulip Festival

celebrate. They also celebrate many different festivals each year. In June, both Montreal and Vancouver host international jazz festivals that bring together famous jazz musicians. Quebec City's Winter Carnival is the largest winter carnival in the world. It features winter parades, snow sculpture contests, and all-night dancing. Ottawa's Tulip Festival celebrates the friendship between Canada and the Netherlands. It is the largest tulip festival in the world, featuring thousands of colorful tulips.

The Calgary Exhibition and Stampede

For ten days each July, things in Calgary in Alberta, Canada get a little wild. It is then that everyone turns into a cowboy or cowgirl to celebrate the Calgary Exhibition and Stampede. The festival includes rodeo competitions, chuck wagon races, carnival rides, clowns, livestock exhibitions, country music, and barrel races.

Each year, about a million people come to the city for the Calgary Exhibition and Stampede. Cowboys and cowgirls from around the world compete in rodeos for prize money. Fans slip into cowboy hats and boots to cheer for their favorite competitors. Everyone loads up on barbecued treats and stacks of pancakes with maple syrup. Soon after the festival ends, Canadians start planning for the next Calgary Exhibition and Stampede to ride into town.

Canada's flag has three wide bands. Two bands are red. One band is white. These are Canada's national colors. In the center of the flag is an eleven-point red maple leaf. The maple leaf is a national symbol of Canada. Canada adopted the flag in 1965.

Canadian money is called the dollar. The exchange rate often changes, but 1.30 Canadian dollars equaled one U.S. dollar in 2003. Like money in the United States, Canadian money includes pennies, nickels, dimes, and quarters.

Count in French

English	French	Say it like this:
one	un	UNH
two	deux	DUH
three	trois	TWA
four	quatre	CAT
five	cinq	SANK
six	six	SEECE
seven	sept	SET
eight	huit	HWEET
nine	neuf	NUF
ten	dix	DEECE

Glossary

curling A sport using a brush and a stone, started in Scotland.

creche (KRESH) A model of the baby Jesus with his parents, visitors, and animals.

mountain range A group of mountains or highlands.

ore (OR) Rock that contains metal, such as iron ore.

petroleum (puh-TROH-lee-uhm) A thick, oily liquid used to make gasoline.

plateau (pla-TOH) An area of high, flat land.

porridge (POR-ij) A breakfast food made by boiling oats until they thicken.

sequel (SEE-kwuhl) A book or movie that continues an earlier story.

sod The top layer of soil that has grass growing on it.

tundra (TUHN-druh) A cold, dry, treeless area of frozen land in the Arctic.

Fast Facts

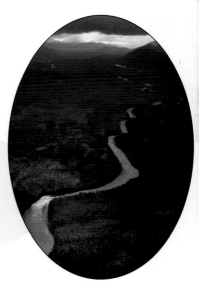

Canada is one of three countries in North America. It is located north of the United States. With more than 3.8 million square miles (9,842,000 square km) of land, Canada is the second-largest country in the world. Russia is the largest.

Canada's motto is "From sea to sea." That is the perfect motto for a country that borders three oceans—the Arctic Ocean, the Pacific Ocean, and the Atlantic Ocean.

The Mackenzie River is Canada's longest river. It is also the third-longest river in the world. It runs 2,635 miles (4,241 km) through Canada's Northwest Territories.

Canada's flag has two red bands with a large white band in between. In the center of the flag is an eleven-point red maple leaf. The maple leaf is a national symbol of Canada.

Canada's average temperatures are 21.6 degrees Fahrenheit (-5.8 degrees C) in January and 70 degrees Fahrenheit (21.1 degrees C) in July. The average rainfall each year is 29.9 inches (75.9 cm).

42

Most Canadians are Christian. Forty-six percent are Roman Catholic and 36 percent are Protestant. Jews, Muslims, Hindus, Buddhists, and Sikhs make up the remaining 18 percent.

Canadian money is called the dollar. The exchange rate often changes, but 1.30 Canadian dollars equaled one U.S. dollar in 2003.

Canada has ten provinces and three territories. Ottawa, in the province of Ontario, is the capital and home to the Canadian parliament.

The highest peak in Canada is Mount Logan. It rises 19,551 feet (5,959 m).

In the center of Canada is the Canadian Shield. It is a rocky area that covers half of Canada's land. The granite rock in the Canadian Shield is 3.5 billion years old.

Most Canadians speak English or French or both. These two languages are the official languages of the country. Canadian children learn both languages in school.

43

Proud to Be Canadian

Samuel de Champlain (1567–1635)

Samuel de Champlain was born in France in 1567. Champlain was a French explorer, navigator, and mapmaker. He explored much of northeastern North America, making maps of the area and charting Canada's lakes and rivers. Champlain also founded and built the colony of Quebec, Canada, as a fur trading post. He took charge of the colony until it was attacked and taken by the British. He returned to Quebec, when the French regained the colony, and became its governor. He died on December 25, 1635, and was buried in Quebec.

Wayne Gretzky (1961–   )

Wayne Gretzky was born in 1961 in Brantford, Ontario. Gretzky grew up to become a hockey legend. Also known as "The Great One," Gretzky played hockey for the Edmonton Oilers (1978–1988), the Los Angeles Kings (1988–1996), the Saint Louis Blues (1996), and the New York Rangers (1997–1999). In his twenty-one-year career, Gretzky led the Edmonton Oilers to four

44

Stanley Cup Championships and earned sixty-one national records. He was named a National Hockey League (NHL) All-Star eighteen times. With Gretzky's trade to the Los Angeles Kings, hockey interest grew in the United States. Because of this, two new NHL teams were formed. Gretzky was elected into the Hockey Hall of Fame on June 23, 1999.

Lucy Maud Montgomery (1874–1942)

Lucy Maud Montgomery is considered one of Canada's most famous authors. She was only a child when her mother died and her father remarried. Montgomery went to live with her grandparents. Throughout her childhood, she used her writing to escape her lonely days and strict grandparents in Cavendish, Prince Edward Island.

Montgomery's first poem was published when she was sixteen years old. But, in 1904, a story idea that she jotted in her journal would soon become a best-selling children's novel called *Anne of Green Gables* (1907). She followed this popular book with seven *sequels*. During her life, Montgomery wrote 22 novels, 500 short stories, a poetry book, 450 poems, and a diary. Her work is loved around the world. To this very day, people from many countries come to Prince Edward Island to visit the places she wrote about in her books.

Find Out More

Books

Canada by Tracey Boora. Bridgestone Books, MN, 2001.

Welcome to Canada by Meredith Costain. Chelsea House Publishers, PA, 2002.

Canada, The Land by Bobby Kalman. Crabtree Publishing Company, NY, 2002.

True Books: Canada by Elaine Landau. Children's Press, NY, 2000.

Web Sites*

www.canada.gc.ca/
The official Web site for the government of Canada

www.koolkids.ca
The first school in Canada's Arctic on the Internet

Videos

An Introduction to Canada, VHS, 24 minutes. Institute for International Business, Minot, ND, 2000.

The Educational Video Group presents: CBC National: A Sense of Country, VHS, 60 minutes. Educational Video Group, Greenwood, IN, 1996.

*All Internet sites were available and accurate when sent to press.

Index

Page numbers for illustrations are in **boldface.**

About the Author

Patricia J. Murphy writes children's story-books, information books, early readers, and poetry. She also writes for corporations, magazines, educational publishing companies, and museums. Patricia lives in Northbrook, Illinois.

Patricia enjoys spending time with her Canadian friends and watching hockey games. Someday, she would like to play ringette and attend the Calgary Exhibition and Stampede.